Once Again

CAROLYN COLE

Quantum Discovery
A LITERARY AGENCY

ISBN
978-1-963254-01-3 (Paperback)
978-1-963254-02-0 (eBook)

TABLE OF CONTENTS

INTRODUCTION

This book reflects on how good the Lord Jesus Christ is, how He will bring you through any situation in your life if you learn to trust Him and have faith in Him regardless of what you might be going through in your life.

When we learn to stand on His word and not be moved, does this mean that we will not sometimes get frustrated, angry, sad, lonely or so many other emotions that we face, not at all but when we learn to turn to Jesus Christ, we can press on in our lives and not give up.

As I write this book, I pray that it will change lives, give hope, and glorify the Lord Jesus Christ, as I share some things from my own experience I pray for peace in the hearts and minds of those who read it.

I give my Lord and Savior Jesus all the praise for pushing me to write this after my other book MY LIFE did not go so well, I gave up on writing, but the Lord has been pushing me over the last couple of days to start writing. I could hear Him speaking saying so you are just going to give up on your dreams of writing.

The main scripture that keeps me going is 2 Corinthians 12: 9-11 which states He said to me," My grace is sufficient for you, for power is perfected in weakness". Therefore, I delight, in weaknesses, in insults, in distresses, in persecutions, in difficulties, on behalf of Christ, for when I am weak, then I am strong. Giving all praise to God.

CHAPTER I

My Eyes Were Opened

*A*s I sit looking back over my life and reflecting how my Lord and Savior Jesus Christ have not only spared my life many times, but have protected, provided, strengthened me, comforted me, gave me peace when I felt like I couldn't or didn't want to go on any longer, I would begin to speak Philippians 4:6 "The peace that surpasses all understanding will guard your hearts and minds in Christ Jesus". Please underline the word All in this statement because it is most important.

Although I am very grateful to my Lord for life itself, I really became grateful when I had a car accident on June 25, 2021, at 3:15 p.m. it was one of the scariest days of my life when a man crashed into me from behind and knocked me forward into a truck injuring me.

As I sat at home after getting out of the hospital of course my human emotions began to set in as with anyone, I began to feel sorry for myself and wondering why this happened to me, I could hear my husband Harold say as he always did before he passed, "why not you" or "why not me". The reason I named this book "Once Again" is because my Lord Jesus has spared my life so many times over the years that words cannot express how thankful and grateful, I am to Him. The good thing about God is He will not allow us to sit and feel sorry for ourselves when different situations happen in our lives. I am so glad He did not leave us in this world all alone, He promised He would leave us an advocate to be with us forever. John 14:16 (NIV).

The more I sit and reflect over my life the more I must thank the Lord for saving my life and bringing me through all that He has brought be through, I started using drugs at the young age 10 years old to be exact, sneaking behind my parents back because I wanted to be grown and not listen or go to school. I wanted to be cool and hang out, this has nothing to do with my parents, I take full responsibility for my actions, the one thing I have learned is to not always blame someone else for your mistakes but to take responsibility for your actions, that is how we grow in life, that is how we grow closer to God and others, that is how we have peace within our hearts, minds and soul. For a long time, I wanted to blame others for my drug addiction because I was so young but I knew right from wrong, I knew what I was doing and before I knew it 19 long years had passed and I was in to deep, so messed up in my mind I had no self-control and I was lost, mind, body, soul and spirit and yet not knowing or realizing it thinking I had it all together and looking good, but in reality I weighed 98 pounds, wore a size 2 pants and it was scary, very scary but those drugs had me blinded to reality.

Over those 19 years I did some things that I am not proud of, and I am so glad my parents never found out about some of the things I was doing. Thank you Lord, they just loved me as any parent would love their child, (1 Peter 4:8 says above all, love each other deeply, because love covers over a multitude of sins) and although I never thought how my actions were hurting them I know now how much it hurt them to watch me go through that time in my life and I really appreciate them just showing love and praying for me because lord knows I sure needed prayer and that was the only thing that was going to help me.

For anyone who is reading this that knows someone going through this same thing or that might be going through this yourself, I want you to know there is hope so please, please, please don't give up, and for anyone who knows someone just show them love and pray for them because that is the most important thing you can do for them.

Jesus has saved and spared my life so many times it's not even funny, being out there in those streets using those drugs make you think you can do anything or beat anyone, you have no fear at all, you might wonder what kind of drugs I was using at 10 years old, I started off with weed and alcohol, then it went to smoking angel dust, cocaine, acid and then crack cocaine and sometimes all of them at the same time. I thank the Lord that I'm still alive I have used all the above things for 12-14 days nonstop with no food or water, I remember one time my husband literality had to hold my head up and pore water down my throat, so I didn't die, it was only by the grace of God that He spared my life thank you Jesus! That is the insanity that people who use drugs go through, the drugs take over your mind, body, soul and spirit, you have no control over what you are doing, you are just trying to get that same feeling you got the first time you used drugs so you are chasing a feeling and you will do anything to get it.

It was so many times in my drug use that I have robbed men for drugs and money after they have fallen asleep from us hanging out smoking dope then I would have to go into hiding for a while, so they didn't see me and kill me. Thank you, Jesus, for all those times you spared my life, I'm putting all of this out praying that it will help save someone's life and Soul.

CHAPTER II

His Grace and Mercy

The things in chapter one was only a few things in my life that the Lord spared my life from some was my own doing and some were at know fault of my own, the Lord Jesus spared my life from 3 burning buildings where I got out in a matter of a minute and right to this day I am afraid of fire, but I have learned that we go through things in life for us to be able to help someone else with our testimony of the things that God has brought us through. James 1:2 says consider it pure joy when we face many trials in our lives, (focusing on the word when, not if but when). The one thing that I have learn and still learning is that when I praise and still give thanks to Jesus regardless of what I go through I'm able to pull the good out of it, there is always good to pull out of everything we face in life when you walk with the Lord because it is only building your character more and more. So always try to look for the good in everything even when life seems hopeless.

I want others to know that people don't just wake up one day and say I want to be a drug addict it just happens if you are not very careful in what you are doing, who you are hanging out with, places you are going and some situations you put yourself in as teenagers, young adults and adults because I know of people who did not start using drugs until they were 50+ years old so there is no age limit for drug addicts.

One thing I have learned is that there is no problem too big for my Lord and Savior Jesus to fix. Genesis 28:15 God says, "I am with you and will watch over you wherever you go, and I will bring you back to this land. I will not leave you until I have done what I have promised you". I have learned that all those times I thought it was me getting myself out of those bad situations I found myself in it wasn't me it was my Lord and Savior Jesus Christ and I thank Him so very much for watching over me and loving me despite myself.

The drugs made me think I was just that cool and slick that I could get myself out of anything I remember one night when me and my friend were going to go out and do what we did to make money which was selling our bodies, that night as we got ready to go something in my mind (Holy Spirit) told me not to go and I stayed home, not long after she left I heard sirens and went outside to see what was happening and she was laying there dead where the guy stabbed her to death and stood there and waited for the police to come get him, he had just gotten out of jail that day and he said "I hate prostitutes and every chance I get I am going to kill one".

My heart dropped and I was so glad that I did not go out that night with her but then again, I felt like if I would have gone with her maybe I could have helped her or we both might have been killed, that was a scary night for me and as I look back, I believe that was the last time I went out selling my body. Thank you, Holy Spirit, for watching over me. Jeremiah 29:11 says" For I know the plans I have for you, Declared the Lord, plans to prosper you and not to harm you, plans to give you hope and a future."

As I am writing this the Spirit of the Lord is bringing different time in my life from those 19 years of drug use, this is how I know that the Lord has me writing this to help encourage someone else's life and to let them know that God has not forgotten about you and there is a God who love and watches over you so don't give up just hang on, my mother use to always say just hang on to the hands of the Lord because God has a plan for your life and He will never leave or forsake you (Hebrews 13:5).

These few things are only a part of my story but I think we all get the picture of the effects of drugs and alcohol, know one asks to be a drug addict or a alcohol, sometimes we make it out and sometimes we don't, I truly believe that those who don't are still with God and that's just my opinion because even before I came to know Christ He was watching over me and taking care of me because I was truly lost, mind, body, soul, and spirit until He made me stand on the corner by my parents church and I remember asking God, why can't I be like those people, why do I have to be a drug addict? I stood on that corner for hours it was like I was frozen and I could not move I watched my parents go in and out of church that day but they didn't see me, oh how I wanted to go in but I looked a hot mess and to tell you just how God works I had gone to church with my parents before on a Holy Communion Sunday and received communion, somehow I would find myself in different parts of San Francisco in front of different churches on Communion Sunday and I would go in take Communion and leave.

That happen to me for years while I was out there in those streets and know one ever said anything to me, they would just serve me my Communion and let me go. Now if that wasn't the Lord guiding me, please let me know what it was because half the time I didn't realize I was in front of the church and really didn't realize it was Communion Sunday, all I can say is that is the Power of Jesus and thank you Lord because no one really wants to live like that but when you are in to deep you become lost.

CHAPTER III

God's Favor

*T*here are so many times in my life when God had grace and mercy on me, in my addiction I lost my two daughters ages 7 and 4 months behind drugs, I went down the street to buy drugs I was only gone for 5 minutes and the house next door caught a fire, my 7-year-old was afraid and called out the window for help. By the time I got back child protective services (CPS) had taken them. Thank God my daughter knew my mother's phone number and thank God my parents were willing to take custody of my girl, they lived with my mother for 4 years. After that I really lost all hope for about a year or two, at that time I had just met my husband of 30 years now and he had gone to work that night and I just had to go buy drugs (insanity). I felt like I had nothing to live for anymore because my girls were gone and I had nothing, my using continued for 4 more years but the good thing about this whole situation I was able to go see my girls and help my mom with whatever they needed that was God's Grace I believe. The state told me I would never get my girls back then I was really lost and feeling hopeless, although I could go see them it just wasn't the same, I felt like I had failed them more then myself, I felt like I had nothing to live for anymore it was a sad and dark time in my life, within those 4 years I had 2 more sons who were 11 months apart in age by my boyfriend who became my husband of 30 years.

Shortly after I had my youngest son I moved to Santa Rosa where my sister lived, I must say that was the best thing that could have ever happened to me, I moved into a shelter which saved my life, I always say God lead me to the shelter and the shelter lead me right back to God. Thank You Lord for knowing what was best for me, I give you all the praise! That shelter taught me how to have better self-esteem, how to parent my children, run my house, manage my money, stay clean from using drugs with narcotics and alcoholics anonymous meetings and so much more, I must say if that shelter was still there I sure would go volunteer there, it was a six month program and right in the middle of the six months, (you will never believe what happen), the state called me and told me because I was doing so well they were giving me my girls back!!! Glory that was only God's Grace, thank you Lord for your Grace and Mercy, for loving me when I didn't love myself, for your guidance and direction.

The reason I am writing all of this because I know it is so many people in this world who is addicted to drugs and alcohol and have lost their way, there children, their homes and so much more, I truly have a passion for the homeless because I have been there and I know that is not the life anyone wants to live, I pray for the homeless all the time and I do what I can for them but I also know that prayer is the most important thing I can do for them. So, if you are reading this just know that there is always someone praying for you and you will make it, God will work it out for you, there is no problem to big or small for the Good Lord to work out. Right after I got my daughters back, I now had 2 daughters and 2 sons, me and Harold got married and we were a happy family, we moved into our own little house and after having 18 months clean, I went to visit someone who was still using and got caught up again using and had to start all over again. I was so embarrassed, and Harold was so mad at me, but he also showed compassion towards me after he came to pick me up and brought me home. That night I ended up getting pregnant with our youngest daughter and I started my recovery program back from the beginning, my cps worker kept telling me I needed to get an abortion, but I do not believe in abortions, so I was about to have 5 children. After she was born I went to school to be a Certified Nurse's Aide, I now was a mother of 5, a wife and a working woman who loved caring for the elderly and terminally ill patients, well once again God spared me I ended up hurting my back for years I was in severe pain and during all of that my father-in-law came to live with us, Harold had not seen his father in over 15 years because of his drug addiction, I didn't tell you but me and Harold met while we were both using drugs, the 1st day we met we never left each other until the day he passed away on September 3, 2017 he was the love of my life, as I look back over my life sometimes I feel like it was God's plan for me to hurt my back in order for me to be able to take care of grandpa Gus, I took care of him for 12 years until he passed in 2005, then my father passed in 2006 and my mother in 2007 and my sister in 2009. Those were some of the hardest days of my life, I'm so glad that my parents were able to see me not using drugs and doing good raising my children, working, and caring for my family. Thank you, Lord! For He knows the plan He has for you!

I am so glad I was able to be there for grandpa Gus, a couple of years before Grandpa Gus passed, we moved to Elk Grove California, and I went back to school to be a Surgical Technician to work in Labor and delivery. I was able to work for one and a half years before I hurt my back again and that time I was totally disabled and couldn't worked any longer, but I am very grateful to God for allowing me that time on my dream job which was to work in the operating room. Thank you Jesus, I have always wanted to work in the operating room but I never thought I was smart enough to make it through school until my husband pushed me to go to school and only by the grace of God I finished school and was allowed to work my dream job for almost 2 years until I hurt my back again and that was it for me as far as working was concerned for me and the doctors. But God promised me He would never leave or forsake me (Hebrews 13: 5) and I must say He has kept His promise.

CHAPTER IV

Test of my Faith

S ometimes our faith gets tested, but I have learned over the last few years to trust Jesus know matter what is going on in my life and for anyone who is reading this you can make it as well if you just keep trusting God.

In 2009 my sister-in-law came to live with us from Florida and she hated it at first but it was either come live with us or go into a nursing home, which I was not going to allow that to happen when she had family, she was in early stages of dementia and she gave me a hard time for the first few years alone with the chronic pain in my back and spine I was suffering from, my husband really starting to get sick with CHRONIC OBSTRUCTIVE PULMONARY DISEASE (COPD), then I found myself taking care of him and his sister, then in 2011 I had to take full custody of my grandson who was a year old and trusting God all the way to get me through it, My Strength Comes From The Lord! Psalm 121:2-8, that was the only way I could have taken care of them but wait in 2015 my sister who was sick with memory loss came to live with us as well because this is where God put her. On Christmas morning as I was watching my family open gifts the Lord showed me a vision of her coming to live with us and I told my husband that my sister was coming to live with us and he said OKAY, by January 14, 2015, she was here just like God showed me in the vision and I truly thank the Lord for the privilege of being able to take care of them all. Between 2009 and 2010 I had 2 major surgeries, on October 18, 2009 the night before my surgery for endometriosis I was Ordained as a Pastor and I started a ministry for young adults and children called Faithful Body of Christ, this ministry was to help our young adults, teenagers and children that they did not have to take the same road in life that I went down and to teach them about Jesus so they didn't get deceived, the Lord told me to just plant the seed and He would do the rest, it was ran out of my home, we did bible study every Wednesday and I preached and taught every Sunday, I didn't collect offerings because it was about there salvation not about money because God provided everything we needed, Thank You Lord. In 2010 I had neck and spine surgery. I must say when you trust and put all your faith in the Lord He will show up and show out, I came out of the hospitals taking care of others and still running Gods Ministry, after a couple weeks because all I knew to do was draw my strength from God, it was only me there left to take care of everyone else, most of my 5 children were in high school, then they moved out into their own lives so all I knew to do was trust the Lord. Jesus says if you have faith the size of a mustard seed you can move mountains, (Matthew 17:20).

As time went on my sister-in-law got sicker, my husband got sicker and my sister got sicker, my back and spine pain got worst, but God in His goodness kept me, and He will keep you as well if you trust Him. (Isaiah 26:3) says, you will keep him in perfect peace, whose mind is stayed on you, because he trusts in you.

For anyone who is reading this when things feel like they are getting out of control and you feel like you can't make it or it feels like it's just too hard to bear just hold on to the hands of the Lord, that's what my mom use to always say, just put your hands in the hands of the Lord and hold on He will get you through.

Well sadly to say my sister-in-law passed away in 2016, my husband passed away September 3, 2017, and my father passed away on September 2, 2006, I must say that was and sometimes still is a hard thing to bare but again God is keeping me and helping me through that grieving process over the last few years. My sister also passed away on March 10, 2021 now just leaving me and my grandson here in the house, my grandson is now 10 years old and all I know to do is teach him to be a good person, to have morals, values, be respectful, honesty and to know God because I cannot teach him to be a man but if I teach him to be a good person in life and to show love because Jesus is love he will be a good man alone with the help of God.

No matter what is going on in your life if you just don't quit and give up you still have a chance of making it, no one ever said life was going to be easy, if it was easy we wouldn't need Jesus and I have to say I CANNOT live without my Lord and Savior in my life, that is a choice you have to make in life, no one can make it for you, you have to look where He has brought you from, how many time He has spared you and brought you out of different situations cause I have to tell you that it wasn't you who got you out of those situations!

We are now in August of 2021 and I must say that everything has been going fine, after my sister-in-law, my husband and my sister all passed my finances were low I was down $6000 each month and still had to pay all the bills for the house for me and my grandson, worrying and sometimes in a panic on how I was going to do it until I had to look back over the years and realize that once again God kept me because nothing got turned off, the bills were paid and sometimes I didn't even know where the money came from, for a while my bills all went to a $0 balance all of them it was mind blowing!! (Matthew 6:31-33) says do not worry, saying, what shall we eat? Or what shall we drink? Or what shall we wear? For the pagans run after all these things, and your heavenly father knows that you need them. But seek first his kingdom and his righteousness, and all these things will be given to you as well. My Lord and Savior has met all the needs of me and my grandson over the years, one thing that I have learned is the Jesus will never fail you, people sometimes fail you, but Jesus will NEVER FAIL YOU!!!

CHAPTER V

"A New Season"

*T*he topic for this chapter is a new season because I am now learning new things that I have not had to do in over 35 years. I now must learn how to be a single parent of a 10-year-old boy, I now must live alone without my husband and still deal with this spine and nerve pain, which is getting worse, but I thank God that my husband taught me how to fix a few things around my house without any help, thank you honey, and thank you Jesus.

I wish I could say as far as my emotions everything was alright but some days are better than others, some nights are better than others, when you have slept in the same bed with the same person for 30 years it's very different when that person is not there any longer, when you are the one who holds everyone else together through their grieving process you put yourself last to make sure everyone like your kids and grandkids are alright, then in those late nights when no one else is around that is when you have to just cry out to God.

Sometimes the smallest things can make you fall apart crying, after my husband passed away I was on the phone making a doctors appointment and the receptionist ask me who was my emergency contact and I fell apart and didn't know what to say, I started crying and I had to tell the lady I would call her back, all of my emergency contacts which was my mother, fathers and my husband Harold had all passed away, I thought in my mind oh God who do I trust with my life in case of an emergency. I have to say that question bothered me for about a week, mind you I have 5 children, but they were not Harold or my mom who I knew would make the best choices for my life, to be honest my mind said which one of these children do I trust that much. LOL (Laugh out Loud).

But only by the grace of God it got a little easier to put someone down as my emergency contact, I have learned and I am learning that things will get a little easier to deal with if you allow the Lord to guide you through your pain, anyone who might be going through this it will get a little easier but it is going to take some time and some work, what I do know is that you do have to put in the work to get past your grieving process, what I do know is that only God can help you through it, only God can comfort you in those late nights when your heart is heavy and hurting, 1 Peter 5:7-9 says cast all your cares upon HIM, for HE cares for you (So True) Thank You Lord for caring for me. Thank You Lord for your guidance and direction each day I give you all the Praise.

In learning a new thing over this past year all I keep hearing in my spirit is the Lord saying total dependance, total dependance on Me, sometimes in our lives we don't have a choice but to be dependent on God when no one else is there and it's only you and the Lord, I am learning all I have is the Lord and that's alright because He promised He would never leave or forsake me (Hebrews 13:5). Although I have gone through so much in my life, I would not change a thing because I would not be the person who

I am today if I was to change one thing, thank you Lord for who you are shaping me to be, Jeremiah 18:6 says O house of Israel, cannot I do with you as this potter? Saith the Lord. Behold, as the clay is in the potter's hand, so are you in my hand.

I must say, others can tell you all day long to seek God and stay focus, but you must see it for yourself, you must make up your mind for yourself if you want to follow God and no one can make that choice for you but you.

Although I am in a new season of my life I wish I could say the trials and suffering stopped but they didn't, they continue to come after my husband (Harold) passed away my doctor gave me 2 different medicines that should not have been taken together, the doctor or the pharmacist did not catch the mistake and I broke out all over my body with blisters from head to toe, I took the medicine for 3 months and no one caught the mistake, right to this day months later I am still trying to get my body right, I now have black marks all over my body from top to bottom. I am so glad that my Lord and Savior promised never to leave or forsake me because I could not do this without Him.

Not only did I have blisters all over, but they itched all the time, sometimes I didn't think I was going to make it because it was unbearable at times it made me think about Job in the bible where Satan put sores all over his body and all that he had gone through in the book of Job chapters 1 and 2. Sometimes some of my friends call me Jobetta from all the things that they have seen me go through in my life and are still going through, reflecting on Jobs situations he never cursed God and that helps me sometimes stay focused because I reflect on how Job must have felt through his suffering. I'm learning to use every situation that I face as a learning experience more and more each day because I know that God is teaching me something and there is a lesson in it.

James 1:2 says consider it pure joy when you face many trials, I'm learning to praise and trust God in every situation I go through because it makes it a little easier to face them when I stand on the word of God.

Whoever is reading this please learn God's word and learn to trust Him and stand on that word it will give you joy, it will strengthen you, it will give you peace, it will teach you to forgive, it will show you how to love others because Jesus is Love.

In this new season I am learning each day to be totally dependent on God, when I talked about my spine and back problems they have gotten worse, when the doctor told me that every disc in my back is bulging and crushing my spine I lost it, because I could not believe that I have taken care of others my whole life and now my body is giving out on me, that devastated me for about a week I had to just process that in my mind, my first thought was who is going to take care of me and how am I going to take care of my grandson, at that time I really had to do some soul searching about my life, then again I began to hear the Lord say total dependance on me, I had to reflect back over my life and began to remember God's promises in the word, the more I did that the stronger I got mind and body, the stronger I am getting every day. As I am writing this, I am facing this trial each day, I wish I could say it is easy, but it is not. Some days are good and some days I am in a lot of pain, but I must press on trusting that God will give me the strength that I need, He promised He would meet all my needs and that is what I stand on each day. Thank you, Lord.

As time goes on, I'm starting to depend on the Lord more and more, I am learning to say the serenity prayer alone with everything else in my life which says, God grant me the serenity to except the things I cannot change, the courage to change the things I can and the wisdom to know the difference, I have learned to line that prayer up with,

Ecclesiastes 3:1-8 which says, there is a time for everything
and a season for every activity under the heavens.

A time to be born and a time to die,

A time to plant and a time to uproot,

A time to kill and a time to heal,

A time to tear down and a time to build,

A time to weep and a time to laugh,

A time to mourn and a time to dance,

A time to scatter stone and a time to gather them,

A time to embrace and a time to refrain from embracing,

A time to search and a time to give up,

A time to keep and a time to throw away,

A time tear and a time to mend,

A time to be silent and a time to speak,

A time to love and a time to hate,

A time for war and a time for peace.

What I have learned is that the secret of God's peace is to
discover, accept and appreciate God's perfect timing for every
activity under the heavens, and to use every situation as a learning
experience because it will only help you to grow and push forward
in your life, sometimes you might feel like you want to give up,
but God will not allow you to give up at all. Thank you, Jesus,
for not letting me give up on myself and my life, it's only by your
grace and mercy that I am still alive and still here.

Each day I sit down and write a little more in this book I
wish I could say that everything in my life is going fine but there
is so much stuff going on in my life and in my families lives that

it's a shame, I always say there is never a dull moment in the cole house, it's always something going on with me, my children, or my grandchildren. For anyone who knows me know that my family is my life and I love them to heaven and back, but in this season of my life I am learning to put my children and grandchildren in the hands of the Lord, I am learning that the battle is not mine. I am learning to pray, move out of God's way and stay out of the situation and watch God's will be done in their lives.

CHAPTER VI

"Moving Forward"

*E*ach day that the Lord allows me to wake up is a new day, a new opportunity, new grace, new mercy, a new anointing over my life, new strength, and new peace in my life. I will never see yesterday again, I'm not promised tomorrow so that is why I am learning to just take it one day at a time, each day is a gift from God that is why it is called the present day that He blessed us to see, to live, to praise, to worship and to be used by God to Glorify God.

For anyone who is reading this take advantage of each day because we don't know if we will see tomorrow, never hold grudges always forgive so you won't be held hostage by your unforgiveness (Mark 11:24-25 Jesus our Lord said that if you forgive, you shall be forgiven. He also made it clear that if you do not forgive men their trespasses, neither will your Father in heaven forgive you your trespasses. And you can be sure that if your sins are not forgiven, your prayers cannot be answered).

As I move forward in my walk with Christ and in my life the Lord has shown me so many different things, so many different revelations through His word and others, scriptures that I have read many times I am getting new revelations to apply to my life for my own purpose. The more I seek the Lord Jesus the more I appreciate Him and His Love for me, I appreciate the beauty around me, the stars, moon, trees, wind, clouds, rain, sun, animals, people. I have learned that everything under the heavens have a purpose as well as me and you. I have learned that God is so amazing, and His Love is unconditional always, when I put my focus on Jesus, I can't help but to see how amazing He really is regardless of what might be going on in my life.

I must say there is never a dull moment in the Cole house, I use to only think it was just my house but it's not, I am so sure that there is never a dull moment in your house as well especially when you are trying to stay and learn how to keep your focus on Jesus and that is not an easy thing to do, but when you learn how to stand on, trust and believe His word and promises it gets easier, things don't affect you like they use to and to be honest life doesn't seem like you can't do this any longer, like you have lost all hope, because we sometimes feel like that when we know Jesus and when we don't know Jesus. When we don't know Jesus, we are searching but we don't know what we are searching for just as I was when I was using drugs all day every day not in my right mind, I was looking for love in all the wrong places, I used drugs to keep from feeling and dealing with my emotion, to take carolyn out of herself (anyone ever felt like this before) that was before I knew the Love (unconditional Love) of my Lord and Savior Jesus Christ.

Sometimes we go through things in our lives for us to be able to help and relate to others in our future, over this last year the Lord revealed to me that all the things I have gone through in my life is to help others, He showed me that I could relate to the drug addicts, the homeless, the teen parents, the parents who have gotten their children taken by child protective service (cps), the prostitutes, those in domestic violence situations, the lonely, those raising grandchildren, those who are grieving, those who have lost their soul mates.

The more I seek the Lord the more I am learning that all of these things are for the benefits of others in order to glorify God so His Glory can be seen, I am learning it has nothing to do with me it's all about glorifying God, the more I realize that the more I understand His will and His purpose for my life the more I can make it through to the other side, the more I can have joy and peace in my life regardless of the situation.

For others who are reading this know that you can make it, I wish I could say it's going to be easy but it's not, you can make it through with God and only in God's strength then in your own strength, this is a personal choice that you have to make up in your own mind that you are going to do this, you are going to keep seeking God regardless of the situation. My prayer for each person who might be reading this book is to never give up, one thing I have learned over the years is I am my worst enemy. I have learned not to listen to my own thoughts if the thoughts are negative ones about myself. Sometimes I just must cry out to the Good Lord for help because He is the only one who can help me make it through the grief, the pain and the loneliness I sometimes feel.

CHAPTER VII

"Rediscovering who you are"

*A*s time has gone by it's been a while since I have last written, I have discovered so much about my life and about who I really am, I am so grateful to God for reminding me who I am, so much has happened in my life over the years that I honestly forgot who Carolyn was, sometimes we know that we know the Lord but because of the trials in life beating us down we forget who we really are.

2 Corinthiaans 4:8-9

Paul says that we are afflicted in every way, but not crushed; perplexed, but not despairing; persecuted, but not forsaken; struck down but not destroyed.

Therefore, regardless of any given situation in our lives when we know what we know, and we trust and believe that GOD is with us through all things that gives us the strength to keep pressing forward in all things.

We sometimes focus on the trials of life, the world, family, jobs, school, addictions that we forget. Lord God Thank You for reminding me who I am in you, thank You for reminding me and for sending the Holy Spirit to open up my mind once again because it doesn't matter what our life style is we were created for a purpose but the only way we can discover our purpose is to seek the all Mighty God, His Way and His Will for our lives and begin to live according to His Way putting our selfish ways, selfish thoughts, selfish attitudes, all of our old ways aside and learning new way to think, live, act. (John 14:6) Jesus says, I am the way the truth and the life know one comes to the Father except through me.

As I continue to rediscover myself and the plan that God has for my life it has been a great joy, I have been so busy learning myself that it has been a couple of months since I last sat down to write until God reminded me that I am loosing balance in my life and that I have to gain balance while starting to walk and live out my dreams and goals, taking time to write, raise my grandson, teaching classes, bible study, ministering to others and learning to just be who I am and who the Lord created me to be.

Giving God all the Praise today it's 5 a.m. and I am sitting here with my mind on Jesus this morning listening to the Lord speaking to me, it has been a minute since, I last sat down to write. The more God reminds me of who I am in Jesus the more trials come my way, the more I began to apply the word of God to my life the more trials come my way. The more I watch my family go through different situations and I watch God bring them through and I still have peace within my mind and my heart the more I discover who I am in Jesus, the more I apply the word of God to my life the more peace and joy I am learning to have regardless of the situation, so much have gone on in my life since the last time

I have sat down to write, I had a major kidney infection, which turned into cellulitis (a blood infection) in my leg and foot then it turned into sepsis (a blood infection which spread through my whole body), I was so sick before I knew I had the kidney infection. I was home with only my three grandkids and began to run a fever of 104 non responsive and I thank God that they knew to call someone when I wasn't responding to them, when I did come to all my children and grandkids were standing around me that evening trying to make me go to the hospital but I wouldn't go for two whole days I thought I just had a flu or something, by day 3 I went and they gave me medicine, but 2 days later my leg and foot had swollen so big it looked like I had elephant Titus, I thought it was just fluid on my leg but it was infection in my whole leg and foot, they gave me more medicine to take it got well but after all the meds were gone a week later it was back and worse. By this time, I was begging them to take me to the hospital, I ended up spending 5 days in the hospital with them giving me 3 different antibiotics in IV 3 times a day. But what I learned is that God was using me to minister to the nurses in the hospital. I have learned and I am learning that weeping may endure for a night, but joy comes in the morning Psalm 30:5. We are now coming up on the Holiday season and I must say it's a hard time of the year for me because I miss my husband, my life is not the same any longer, everything has changed but God is still Good, God is still worthy to be praised, each day that I continue to trust God (Jesus), learn what my purpose is in life and keep pressing forward I will not lose, although each day is different I still choose to press on regardless of the situation in my life or my families lives some days seem better than others but I am learning to choose to make everyday a good day. It's all about how you want your day to be, you get to make the choice, it's all about if you choose to have a good day or a bad day and I choose to speak life, health and strength over my mind, body, soul, and spirit.

CHAPTER VIII

"A New Beginning"

*I*t has been a minute since I have written in my book, so much has gone on in the last couple of months not only in my life but, also in my families lives but one thing I have learned is that when we make up in our minds that we are not going to quit seeking and praising God or allow anyone to take our peace or joy. When we decide that we are not willing to give it up and we are going to trust that God will work everything out for our good and on our behalf it helps us to press on, Sometimes when we think things are bad are we are in a bad situation just remember what (Romans 8:28) says, we know that in all things God works for the good of those who love him, who have been called according to his purpose. There is always good in every bad situation and once we realize that and learn to pull the good out it makes things a little easier.

Over the last couple of years I have learned that it is my time to live for me (Carolyn), I have learned that my children's battles are not mine but the Lords and they have to learn to seek God for themselves now that they are adults and I must say that sometimes it's not an easy thing to do when you see your children hurting or going through some things in their lives but the more you try to help and bail them out the more you are in God's way for Him to have His way and get their attention. One thing I do know is that the moment I made up in my mind that I wasn't giving up my peace anymore all hell broke loose within my family, yes I love my children but I also love God and sometimes when I just move out of God way and don't get involved in their situations they begin to fill like I don't love them anymore but one thing I have learned is that is a normal feeling no matter how old your children are, I remember feeling like that when my father would not step into my situation and just put me and my situation in God's hands I honestly remember feeling like he didn't love me any more until I realized it was for my own good and then I appreciated it and realized it had nothing to do with him loving me. so, when you see your children going through different situations in life learn to back up and get out of God's way keep them in prayer, keep loving on them even if you must love on them from a far that's alright too.

Although there has been so much going on I can still see the good that is coming out of these things, I can see change in my children's lives, I don't know if they can see the change in their own lives, but I can see change happening.

I can also see growth in my own life for the better, I see God answering some of my own personal prayers that I thought would never happen. One thing that I am learning is that when you pray for something never doubt God because He is able to do immeasurably more than we can ask for or even imagine. (Ephesians 3:20), when I sit and think about the goodness of God all I can say is.

God, "You are something else." Glory to the Highest God. The more we began to allow God to have His Way with us then He begin to remove all the old stuff from our minds and hearts, stuff like unforgiveness of ourselves and others, selfishness, hurt hearts, pride, jealousy, and all those dark secrets that we hold on to that only God know about. When we become open and available to Him, His way and His Will then and only then will be able to forgive and love ourselves, we will be able to let go of some of that stuff that is holding us hostage in our minds and turning it over to God allowing Him to remove it from our thoughts. (Romans 12:2) says we are to be transformed by the renewing of our minds. One thing that I have learned is that we must work at that daily to continue to renew our minds it's not a one-time thing and stop it's daily. Anything that we want we must work at it because (practice makes perfect),

The more I trust God and depend on Him the more my mind change, the more I begin to love myself, the more I want to know more about who Jesus is, the more I want to walk in His ways and not my own, the more I trust Him the better I feel about myself, and the better I feel about myself the more I began to Love the Lord Jesus, and the more I began to love myself the more I think about just how much He really loves me and how deep His love goes for me, how high, how wide, how far, how deep that love that the one and only God has for me. put yourself in that place and just think about it. That love that Jesus gives us is so amazing you can't even describe how good it is or how good it makes you feel there is no words to describe it, it is beyond amazing that's that agape love unconditional, never judging, always forgiving, always caring for us morning noon and night. (I LOVE JESUS). Over the last couple of months I have watched him answer some prayers with my finances, one big prayer that He has answered for me is he is bringing a friend back in my life who I never thought I would ever see again and out of the blue he text me and said he was coming back home because he moved away a few years ago and I am so excited and I can't wait to see him, he has always been a part of my family and I was so hurt when he left, this person always watched over me and took care of me even at my husbands request after my husband got really sick he would always tell this friend to go with me wherever I had to go and not to let anything happen to me. I have much respect for this person because he did what my husband asked him to do, he was always there when my husband asked him to be there. So, to my friend I just want to say thank you for being there not only me but for my whole family. This is prayer number 2 that God has answerer there is still 1 bigger one that he promised me. God promised me 3 prayers He was going to give me He is working on number 2 right now my friend is on the way, and I can't wait to see him. The 3rd prayer is to follow, and I know it because I trust God He has never lied or forsaken me, and I trust what he says. I am learning never to doubt God anymore because he has been good to me. It has been a couple of days since I have written, I am happy to say that my friend has arrived and I am so happy it was everything that I expected that moment as I opened that door and he was standing there the love between two friends was back like we had never been apart, thank you God for answering not only my prayer but for answering both of our prayers. I thought I was the only one excited, but it turned out that he was just as excited because he drove 22 hours nonstop to get here as we talked on the phone all night while he was driving. I must say it was so amazing the excitement of him getting closer and closer was amazing, it was like we just picked up where we left off when he left. The closer he got the more excited I became; my heart was beating so fast that I almost couldn't take it about.

6am he told me to lay down and take a nap cause I had to go to church so I did and slept at about 5 minutes and dear God when he called and said he was 8 minutes away I couldn't take the pressure my heart was beating so fast and by this time I had gotten dressed for church I trying to make sure I looked okay and the pressure was on, I heard the dog bark when he pulled in the driveway and I told myself that I'm not going to the door until he rings the doorbell and when that doorbell ring my heart was beating so fast it was crazy. When I opened that door I couldn't take the pressure, as he came in when we hugged, we both took a deep breath at the same time it was amazing, it was like we could both now relax we were back together once again. God is so Amazing I can't live without Him because He knows what's best for our lives, again He said for I know the plan I have for you. (Jeremiah 29:11). One thing I know is when He reveals His plan for your life to you it is always amazing, and it is always surprising that it always blows your mind. The more we seek God the more He becomes available to us in every way possible, I love those late-night meetings that I have with Him, and you can have those meetings with the Highest God the Creator of all things the Judge of all men. Those nights are so special, so uplifting, so precious, so intimate and what you want is an intimate relationship. I have learned over the years that that is the most important relationship that you could ever have in your life is an intimate relationship with the Highest God the Lord and savior Jesus Christ. He always keeps His promises that He promise you, I must say that over the last month since He started showing up answering prayer, I have not been this happy in a long time. Not only have I been happy He stepped in and has made all my family accept my new relationship, and they are truly happy for me. I am so grateful to Jesus that my siblings are happy for me as well and I give all the praise to my Lord and Savior Jesus Christ.

CHAPTER IX

Understanding God's Will

*A*s time goes on the more, I began to understand God's will for my life because I want you to understand that God is able to go anything, He can and will answer your prayers. The one thing is that we have to learn how to wait on His timing because our timing is not His timing, the reason that I wrote about my life is because I know my life is a testimony and that it can help others who are facing some of the things that I have gone through so they can have hope in their lives and so they can know that they do have a future and their lives are not over, sometimes it might feel like your life is over and there is no hope and know help in your future but, I am here to tell you that there is hope in Jesus Christ.

Know it's not always easy to have hope when it seems like things are falling apart all around you but when we surrender our will over to God seeking His way and His will for our lives (Matthew 6:33) says seek first the kingdom of God and His righteousness and all these things will be added on to you. Make it a point to study and meditate on this scripture learning it and allowing it to minister to your heart alone with all the other scripters that is in this book and all the other ones that the Lord will put on your heart to minister to you because He loves you very much.

There has been so much going on in my life since the last time I wrote anything, as I explained about my friend coming to stay well, I am happy to tell you that my friend is now my husband, we got married after a week of him being here. God is so good to me and has always kept His promises to me, He has never failed me since I could remember for, He is not a man for which He should lie, He is the King of Kings, and the Lord of Lords, He loves us more than we can imagine and He cares for us and He cares about the things we care about, now that's a good God to care about the things that we care about.

Well, it's been 3 weeks since my friend has arrived and I am happy to tell you that my friend is now my husband, (GOD IS SOMETHING ELSE) . I am happy to say that we got married a week after he arrived the very next Sunday we were married. I give all the Glory to my Lord, my rock, my foundation Jesus Christ. I laughed at my children saying that they just needed to adapt to the marriage and to be honest I am still adapting to the whole thing because I never thought I would see this happening I did not know how this was even possible and I have to tell you that when God makes you a promise, He keeps it there is not one time that I can remember Him not keeping His promise that He made, there is not one time that I can recall Him failing me in any aspect of my life. I now look to my future in what God has in store for me and my new husband that He promised me because I never thought that I would ever see this man again even though God told me that he would be my next husband it's so crazy that when Jesus spoke this to me I heard it, I believed it and I let it go after he moved away never in a million years did I see this coming, although after my husband (Harold) passed away I have to say that I did think about him wondering what was going on in his life, I sometimes looked at his face book page to see what I could see in those moments when I was thinking about him. The more I reflect on how this all took place and how God worked this out the more it feels like a true love story that you read in a book or watch on television, and it just keeps showing me that nothing is impossible for God. now it's time to focus on my future I am so excited to see what God has in store for my future, this is truly a new journey, the song says, "it's another day's journey and I'm glad". One thing that I have learned is that everyday is a new journey in our lives, it's a gift from God and a new opportunity that He has Blessed us with. I am learning more and more that life it too short to not live each day like it's your last, we should never take it for granted, we should never take each other for granted because tomorrow is not promised to any of us so everyday appreciate the things you have the people you have in your lives, look at the beauty in everything and everyone you see, if you don't have a lot of material things thank God for what you do have, if you are facing health challenges thank God that you are still alive, if you don't have family thank God for the people that are in your lives, never stop hoping, never stop dreaming, never stop loving, never stop praising God, never stop seeking God, always be open and available to God, always encourage yourself and don't wait for others to encourage you, stay prayerful always. Understand that there is nothing to hard for God if you make yourself open and available, you might ask yourself how you should do that? By allowing Him to use you in every aspect of your life, begin to practice listening for Him to speak to you in that soft sweet voice, understanding that God will never tell you to do something that you know is not right, that voice in your head that sometimes tells us when we are about to make a bad choice and it reminds you that you know that is wrong don't do that, well that is God speaking to you trying to guide you to do the right thing and all you have to do is listen and be patient because God knows all things and see all things there is nothing that we can hide from Him.

CHAPTER X

"The Beginning of a New Journey"

To my readers, my family and my friends it has been a couple of months since I have sat down and began to write again so much has gone on in these last couple of months since I got married, although we were friends we have never lived together and I have to say it has been a journey for the both of us but God is Good and He is Good All The Time regardless of the situation I draw my strength for the Lord daily. I'm learning how to balance my life all over again alone with everything else I have going on in my life. I am now a new wife Who would have ever thought it after being married the last time for 30 years. One thing I do know is that God doesn't make mistakes and He know the plan He has for our lives we must once again be open and available to His Will and His way of doing things. I am learning all over again to demonstrate God's Love by thought word and deed to my husband because Jesus is Love! As is conclude this book I pray that every reader began to walk in Love, trust

God in every aspect of your life, stay Open and Available to God's will, surrender your thoughts and will over for His Will and His Thoughts while He began to change your life. I SPEAK TOTAL HEALING AND RESTORATION OVER THE MINDS, BODIES, SOULS, AND SPIRITS OF EVERY PERSON THAT PICK THIS BOOK UP!

AS YOU END THIS BOOK, PLEASE WAIT FOR THE NEXT BOOK TO FOLLOW.

THIS BOOK IS SOLELY ABOUT THE GOODNESS OF GOD, HOW AMAZING AND AWESOME HE REALLY IS REGARDLESS OF ANY GIVEN SITUATION WE FIND OURSELVES IN AT ANY GIVEN TIME IN OUR LIVES.

THIS BOOK COVERS ALL PARTS OF LIFE FROM SELLING DRUGS TO BEING A DRUG ADDICT, TO BEING A TEENAGE PARENT WHOSE CHILDREN WERE REMOVES BY (CPS) CHILD PROTECTIVE SERVICES, TO HOMELESSNESS AS WELL AS SELLING MY BODY TO SUPPORT MY HABIT AND HOW MANY TIMES THE LORD JESUS HAS SPARED MY LIFE OVER THE YEARS AND SO MUCH MORE.

THIS BOOK WILL SURELY TEACH US THAT THERE IS NOTHING THAT WE CAN DO TO SEPARATE US FROM THE LOVE OF GOD, THE CREATOR OF ALL THINGS IF YOU JUST TRUST HIM.

AFTER READING THIS BOOK YOU WILL UNDERSTAND THAT THERE IS NO GREATER LOVE THEN THAT OF THE LORD JESUS CHRIST.